HEARTFELT
Thoughts

By Ruth M. Clancy

ImagineWe Publishers
A Global Publisher

If you purchase this book without a cover, you should be aware that this book may have been stolen property and reported as "unsold and destroyed" to the publisher. In such a case, neither the author nor the publisher has received any payment for this "stripped book."

Published by ImagineWe, LLC
ImagineWe Publishers
247 Market Street, Suite 201
Lockport, NY 14094
United States
www.imaginewepublishers.com

© 2025 ImagineWe, LLC

All rights reserved. No part of this publication may be reproduced, stored in a retrieval system, or transmitted in any form or by any means, electronic, mechanical, photocopying, recording, or otherwise without the prior permission of the publisher or in accordance with the provisions of the Copyright, Designs and Patents Act 1988 or under the terms of any license permitting limited copying issued by the Copyright Licensing Agency. For permissions, write to the publisher "Attention: Permissions Coordinator" at info@imaginewepublishers.com.

ISBN: 979-8-9917997-8-2 (Paperback)
ISBN: 979-8-9917997-9-9 (Hardback)
Library of Congress Control Number:

First Edition

We are always looking for new authors. For more information, please visit the website listed above. To shop our selection of books and merchandise you can visit: shop.imaginewepublishers.com

I would like to dedicate this book of poetry, first to my Heavenly Father, who blessed me with the talent to write it. I also want to dedicate it to the late Kirk D Vogel, who was the love of my life, and about whom most of the love poems in this book are written. Also, I lovingly want to thank my daughter, Tela R Clancy, for all of her love, support, and inspiration over the years.

Last, but by no means least, I wish to dedicate Heartfelt Thoughts to all of the wonderful people, family, friends, and acquaintances, who have shown me so much love and inspiration throughout my life.

CHAPTER ONE
Sorrow & Grief

At times in life, we find ourselves completely overwhelmed by a loss. We experience sorrow, grief, and despair over things outside of our control. The way to deal with these feelings is simply to experience them, allow ourselves to move through them, and find creative outlets to express them. I have experienced many losses in my life and one thing that has helped me to deal with them is to put pen to paper and write. Hence, I have the following poems to share with you.

Lovingly.

I smile at you... lovingly,
Hoping you don't see the sorrow in my eyes,
As I watch your body wither and fade.
You smile back at me... lovingly,
Knowing that, before a lot of time goes by,
You will be gone... but not from me.
You will stay forever vivid in my memories,
And deep within my heart... lovingly.

Sometimes.

Sometimes the past creeps up and brings tears to your eyes,
And gnaws at your soul, leaving your heart to sink,
And your face to sag.

Perhaps for just a day, maybe two,
Resolution may come ... or not.
Either way, life lingers in the dead of winter, in the sunshine
And the snow.
New footprints appear that lead to spring.

Once again... and again... and again,
Smiles and laughter will come and go,
As will fond memories of rainbows and flowers.

Yet, no matter what the season,
Sometimes the past may creep up
And leave you aching and shivering amidst your thoughts,
Staring at your fears through tear-filled eyes,
One more time.

Depression.

That deep, dark, aching; that hollow feeling that somehow
Springs forth into streams of tears.

I hear you, my dear one, I hear your fear, your wailing,
You're longing for an embrace when no one is there.

You don't want to die, yet the pain's harshness
Has snuffed out your desire to live.

You've prayed and you've begged,
But your miracle doesn't come.
And they tell you that you are in charge of your own happiness,
But they don't say how, or gently guide you towards any light.

They just tell you about the flaws
That rips your wounds deeper.

And my tears fall too, for you, my dear one,
Because, once upon a time, I've felt that deep, dark, aching,
And it is oh, so sad when even those who should, don't understand.

Ruth M. Clancy

"Wipin' The Tears Away."
(song lyrics)

If there's one thing I've learned in the years that I've been livin',
If there's just one thing I can say,
It's that I know how to pick up the pieces of a broken heart,
And wipe the tears away.

So, don't worry 'bout me as I struggle with these feelings,
I struggle with these feelings day to day,
But I'll be alright, I know how to fight,
And I can wipe the tears away.

Yes, I long to be near you, and I miss your voice on the phone,
And, yes, it's hard not to endear you, when I'm all alone.

But you can't lose somethin' that you never had,
So you see, my tears are in vain,
And though I would welcome a bright sunny day,
I've gotten quite used to the rain.

Well, I'm taking care and I'm standing up strong.
Though I'm losin', I'm finding my way,
But somehow I can't stop thinking of you,
And wipin' the tears away.

Yes, I'm taking care and I'm standing up strong,
Though I'm losin', I'm finding my way;
But, somehow, I can't stop thinking of you,
And I can't remember ever feeling this shade of blue,
And it's getting harder in all that I do,
To wipe the tears away.

The Meeting.

You sat there, mouth quivering, holding back anguish,
Holding back tears, speaking oh so softly,
Like a very small tree in the wind,
Your thin branches breaking inaudibly.

"What can we do?" they asked.
"I don't know," you answered, after a long pause,
And in almost a whisper.

Life isn't fair, you know all too well.
You look to me for answers –
"Help me!" you cry.
I can't help you, my Sweet; I do all that I can.
I don't know all the answers.

You sat there, pathetically, like a wilted flower,
And with tears and frustration in my eyes,
My heart broke.

Ruth M. Clancy

For Your Birthday, Mom.

I tied your birthday card onto a helium balloon,
And let it go to heaven with the fullness of the moon.

The birds had hushed their singing,
and your world was turning gray
And, finally came the moment, when there was nothing left to say.

My life goes on each morning... to where I just don't know,
And every day there are teardrops because I miss you so.

Someday these floods of sorrow may turn to gentle rain...
I'll embrace all you have given, and that joy will ease the pain.

But today the rolling thunder and the beauty that is real
Can't take away this aching in the midst of all I feel.

I see you in the sunlight, and your aura makes me smile,
But I must bear this sadness, for however long a while.

I know you want me to be happy as I watch this setting sun,
But you know that I was always the frightened, lonely one.

Please forgive the times I've hurt you, please forgive me if I cry.
Please know how much I love you, how much I hate to say goodbye.

I know this is kind of crazy, but it's the best that I can do,
To send this card to heaven, with my clinging love for you.

Losing Mom.

The last time I saw her, the moon was a silvery sliver,
And there was a shiny teardrop in the corner of her eye.
And though the time was nearing, the little girl inside of me
Did not believe that she would really die.

And now, in January, I feel so cold and empty;
It's hard to move and harder to keep still,
So I just let my heart sink, as I blow out the lighted candle
That glows next to her picture on the window sill.

My mother always loved me,
In a way that no fine words can ever explain;
And I'm forever grateful, but my gratitude
Doesn't seem to ease the pain
Of not having her here -- of not having her near.

It was late in autumn when she left my life forever,
Beckoned by the sweetness of the angels' song,
And though I'm happy that she's joyful now,
As I shiver tearfully out of my numbness,
I'm wondering if spring will ever come.

You see, I'd like to tend my garden to magnify life's beauty,
Maybe plant some lovely flowers in her name;
But some kind of strange foreboding
keeps reminding all my dreams
That life for me will never be the same.

Summer Rain.

Summer rain coming down, trying to ease my pain,
Wet, green grass and leaves shining through the dusk
Of my troubled heart...

And where am I to go in this summer rain,
Near the end of July in all its pain - why is it so?

The drops cool my skin, relieving a tense burden,
A burden that I carry alone,
Where there is no one to love me
Now that you're gone.

The Morning You Died.

I got the call... I hadn't been able to be with you when it happened,
When you took your last breath.

I felt numb as I walked into the room
And saw your lifeless body, but ever so gently,
The tears began to fall.

I spoke to you softly,
As if a part of you was still there.

I kissed your cool forehead and touched your cold hand.
Then, I whispered a promise to you one last time:
"Always and forever..."

My 'Angel' Kitty.

I found an 'Angel' hair today; I looked it over and held it in my hand.
It was black and white and gray, and I stroked it with my finger;
But, as I sighed, it blew away, like a tiny grain of sand.

She was my roommate and my friend; she was my teacher, and my child,
And from God's heaven, He did send this lovely creature to and for me,
Though it seems now like too short a while.

Her ears were tall and her tail was long, her markings beautiful to see;
Spun gold fur with stripes of brown, a white triangle on her face,
A masterpiece, like a perfect song, her colors meshed in harmony.

She was so curious and wise, playful, silly, and a pain,
With big, round, yellow, black-rimmed eyes,
loud, long purrs, and gentle cries,
But I will never hear her, or see her, or touch her again.

Yes, I found an 'Angel' hair today, and fond memories filled my mind;
The laughter doesn't fade away, nor does the love and joy.
And in my heart, she'll always stay, my sweet, one-of-a-kind.

In Between.

Who's being born and who is dying; is that what it's all about?
And everything in between? I want to stay awhile,
Here in my life, here in my grief.

So, many here and so many there,
And no one is in between, except for the dying;
And, oh how hard and awful it must be, that in-between place,
Where love and pain, both tear at you, like vicious beasts
That won't let go until it's time.

Ruth M. Clancy

Planting Flowers.

Crying like a little girl, my middle-aged heart breaking,
"I just can't go there,"
I told my brother, as he stood by me, his own heart aching.
So he kissed me goodbye and
promised he'd plant them on their grave,
Those daffodils and tulip bulbs that, in full trust, I gave.

I went there with Dad one time; my brother does not know;
But I won't forget that summer's day a couple years ago,
When my dad and I stood there and sang "Amazing Grace"
And he said a prayer of gratitude,
while tears streamed down my face.

Then we hugged and cried together on that cemetery hill,
And we left Mom's birthday flowers,
hoping she would see them still.
Now, Dad lies there with her and it causes me such pain,
That I don't know if I'll ever go back to that place again.

Maybe in the springtime, I'll view it from afar
And look for colorful flowers from the window of my car,
And see that my brother planted what I could only bring,
And perhaps I'll say a grateful prayer and try my best to sing.

For Kristy.

Today is your birthday, and I miss you so.
Though you left this earth years ago,
Your song and your laughter still ring in my ears,
And words that you said still bring me to tears.

You were one of a kind, you were one of God's own,
And I'm so happy to know you now kneel at His throne,
Yet my heart hasn't forgotten the time you were here,
The love that you shared with all you held dear.

Yes, there are so many who miss you today,
But we all wish you, in Heaven, a Happy Birthday!

Just Be.

"... Consider the lilies of the field, how they grow; they toil not, neither do they spin. And yet I say unto you, that even Solomon in all his glory was not arrayed like one of these." Matthew 6:28 & 29, KJV

You are beautiful, just as you are,
no matter what you may or may not do.
Mom told me, not long before she died, that I do so much,
And when I responded that I really didn't do that much (for her),
She said to me, "It's not what you do; it's who you are."

She was so beautiful in so many ways,
always seeming to see the goodness in others,
But not in herself.
She struggled so hard and suffered so much.
I don't think she ever fully realized how
strong and good and beautiful she was.

I truly hope she knows it now...
I love her and miss her so!

Mother's Day.

I see her smile and the love in her eyes;
I even remember the comfort of her lap,
And the creaking rhythm of the rocking chair.

When she lay dying, there was a single teardrop
In the corner of her eye, and there was a sunbeam,
Beaming through the clouds over the hospital.

Oh, how she suffered those last weeks!
It broke all our hearts into pieces.
And, when she left, there was such a huge void.

She brought so much to her family;
She gave so much to me, and so,
after all the years she's been gone,
I still see her smile and the love in her eyes,
And my tears flow down, on Mother's Day.

A Mourning Heart.

I mourn for a life left behind,
for another love that was blind,
With the wind softly whispering, "Where now?"
And a prickling fear,
Asking how to move beyond,
So I sink deep into my sofa without a tear,
Trying not to be sorry;
And there's no use in asking why,
Or in wondering what tomorrow will bring;
I'm just here, like a fly... on the wall.

Happy Birthday, My Friend.

I'm so happy it's your birthday,
for all the love and laughter you gave away.
You had more than your share of suffering and strife,
But I am so glad you were in my life!

From the time we were children until the very end,
Though far away, you were always a good and faithful friend.

And I'm so happy it's your birthday,
though it probably matters to you no more;
But to me, it means memories of warm hugs and smiles,
Of talking and laughing over time and between the miles.

And so I wish you "Happy Birthday"
'cause in my heart, you'll never be gone.
Through bittersweet tears, I'll remember the years
Of friendship and good, old-fashioned fun.

What She Gave.

She gave me stories, she gave me songs,
a yet strong hand to climb upon.
She gave me gentle guidance when ere I came;
we made a joyful rhythm with her cane.
She shared her time, which wasn't long,
with a little girl who felt alone,
And as I stood before those big, white doors,
I knew her arms too were outstretched for more.

Then came that ever-painful day
those doors didn't open right away,
And I stood wanting and confused,
knocking, wailing, and not enthused
By other's words of why or how
I couldn't enter that room right now.
And when I finally did, she wasn't there,
just her silent cane on the back of a chair,
And though I tapped it on the floor,
it made no rhythm anymore.
I wanted to go wherever she'd gone,
to the big blue sky, white clouds and sun;
Or wherever she and Jesus were,
but I never again could be with her.

And the little girl's heart silently broke in two,
Without understanding, or knowing what to do,
So she did what she could up through the years
to freeze the pain and hide the tears.
She learned to want and she learned to cling
to many an unworthwhile thing;

And, as a woman, strove to start
filling the emptiness in her heart.
Sometimes she hung on so tight
and so strong that any time with her seemed too long,
Or she'd pass right by a loving smile,
afraid of it leaving in too little a while.
And though her heart was a precious stone,
it thrived on the pain of being alone.

I was just about two when Aunt Deltie died;
I don't remember if I cried,
But my time is passing, and none too slow,
And it's time for the scared, lonely girl to let go
Of the confusion, the fear, the pain,
the tears that she's carried with her all these years,
And cling instead to the song,
to find her own strength to climb upon,
To take God's hand when she needs a guide,
and find joy and rhythm from inside;
To share her time, whether short or long
and to never have to feel alone;
Knowing that there are always outstretched arms for me,
And embrace myself with dignity.

Sweet Peonies.

"Well, I called up a neighbor this morning," said he,
"Cause in their yard were oodles of sweet peonies,
Like the kind decorating the church in forty-one,
Where my love and I married at twenty-four years young."

"I asked if they'd mind if I picked some today.
I just needed enough for a couple bouquets.
One to put next to her picture inside,
And one to place by the headstone of my beautiful bride."

"Take all you want," the neighbor had said,
So he'd picked up his cane and gone right ahead.
He had gathered the flowers, some pink and some white,
And arranged them together, his sorrow to spite.

Well, I went there to see him, despite my own fears,
Where I saw the old man keeping guard o'er his tears,
And I touched and I smelled those sweet peonies
On the day that would have been their 64th anniversary.

I listened to his stories of love and of life,
But mostly about his wonderful wife.
They had kept their vows -- "till death do us part,"
And I began to feel the man's broken heart.

When finally I left him, I turned back around
And went to the cemetery, where quickly I found
The sweet peonies in a vase by her stone –
I touched them and smelled them and cried there alone.

I could not hold back all the feelings inside,
As I stood at the grave of his beautiful bride,
Because, like him, I knew there would be no other
Like his beautiful bride -- like my beautiful mother.

CHAPTER TWO
Love

Love can be a very complicated subject. For some, at various times in our lives, it can be a very sad subject. But for a few of us, love can bloom into something spectacular and special, and can last a lifetime. Many of the following are poems about that kind of true love. I hope you enjoy them.

Until Now.

How do I begin to describe a love
I never thought was possible for me... until now,
A kinship like I've never known,
a deep caring I could never own... until now.
Now, I am in your arms, in your heart, and in your dreams.
Back when 'love' was painful, it wasn't love at all,
But now it gives a warm and happy glow,
now it comes from you and me,
Realizing our love together and for each other.

It comes from best friends, who would never think of betrayal,
And from sweet, sensuous kisses that mean nothing more,
And nothing less, than true love and compassion.
It comes through faith, confidence, and trust.
It comes from a mission of one never wanting to hurt the other;
It comes from mutual respect and friendship.
It comes from Love itself because it comes from God.

It is a gift, a blessing, a joy that you and I have been given.
It is also a responsibility to nurture and cherish.
This love is neither a fairytale, nor a passing fancy, but a reality,
A truth that came to call when we were yet strangers;
And now it comes to embrace both of us each day:
A beauty, a joy, a peace,
a sense of home that neither of us has ever had...
Until now.

Ruth M. Clancy

The Words.

Can't take back the words once they've been said,
Can't hold back the heart, once it dominates the head,
And that is why, my sweetest friend,
I am so afraid to say, "I love you."

I've lost so much in love, more than you can ever know,
So please try to forgive me, when I try to tell you so...

I never want to go back to that dark and lonely place
That has happened before, when I misread a smiling face,
Or thought some sparkling eyes portrayed an open door.

But I've never felt so warm and peaceful next to anyone,
Never felt such strong beginnings from a rising sun,
And when the storm prevails, I can always find shelter
Waiting in your arms, ready to hold me close, and not falter.

Sometimes I feel it from the center of my being,
from the bottom of my soul;
Sometimes it takes all my energy, all my self-control
Just not to say... that I feel this way.

Whatever this is we have, I believe it is a gift from up above,
As surely as autumn's changing leaves, as surely as love is love.
Still, I can't find the words, as life's breezes gently blow,
As life's voices softly tell me what is true.
I still can't seem to say... that I love you,
No matter how I want to speak it, amidst this ebb and flow.
Still, for some unknown reason, I just want you to know...
That I do.

Ruth M. Clancy

What You've Done.

Just when I thought I'd never be ready, you came along to care.
Just when I'd decided to find a hiding place, you were there.

And I can't stop being who I am,
but I don't think I have to anymore,
'Cause here I am, standing next to you and this open door.

Autumn leaves and roses, together surround us,
And the cold winds of the past want to gather 'round us...

But I've never felt such overwhelming warmth inside,
Not always looking backward for a place to hide.

Thank you for seeing into my eyes and not running away;
Thank you for holding my hand.
I wish that you could see into my heart,
'Cause I think that you alone might understand...
The brokenness there -- You've already touched it;
Allowed me to really smile and go on.

A gentle, rippling river, glistening in the sun,
Life rolling on, like a sea of sparkling diamonds:
That's what you've done...
To my lonely soul.

A Perfect Color.

Being in your arms is such a perfect color,
like a summer's gentle breeze,
Like the mighty ocean's roar; and the sweetness in your eyes
Shines for me like no other, reminding me every day of rainbows
along the way,
Rainbows that have led me to your door
-- and laughing in the rain,
Loving through the storm is so much more than possible,
With your smile to keep me warm.

So let's not forget that together
we can stand and walk through anything,
As long as we walk hand in hand; and if one of us should fall,
We need not blame the other, because being in each other's arms
Is such a perfect color.

Ruth M. Clancy

Beside Me.

I'm not sure what this is,
and I've been on this earth for quite awhile.
I just know that you turn me on and make me smile,
Like nothing I've ever known before,
like nothing I may ever know again
In this life.

You are someone I can trust with all my dreams and despair.
Wherever I turn my thoughts, you are standing there,
Ready to hold me close, ready to take me in,
Into your life.

There's so much going on all around this heart of mine,
But one thing is for sure, you've a place in time
Within it.
There's so much I can't say, 'cause my words trip over fear,
But I know that I won't run, as long as you are here
Beside me.

"You Made Me Feel."
(song lyrics)

Softly, like a gentle autumn rain
Warmly, like the sun upon my skin,
Lovely, like a rainbow in the sky,
You made me feel.

Suddenly, like lightning in the dark,
Joyfully, like the singing of a lark,
And powerfully, like water bursting through a dam,
You made me feel.

Ooh-o oooh

And I became flooded with the sorrow that came
From the truth about all you could not give to me,
But I stumbled forward, as the tears that I cried
Mirrored a new world that finally I let myself see.

And thankfully, I saw a true friend in your eyes,
Finally, a smile that wasn't a disguise,
And, surely, though I can hope for nothing more,
I know you're real.

And softly, like a gentle autumn rain,
Warmly, like the sun upon my skin,
Lovely, like a rainbow in the sky,
You made me feel... ooh- ooh- ooh,
You made me feel... ooh- ooh- ooh
I know you're for real; you made me feel.

Apprehension.

I don't know how to show you how I feel about you,
And I don't know what to say...
I'm so afraid of falling off the cliffs of yesterday,
But I'm thinking maybe you can show me a new way.

I don't want you to take me wrong -- I don't want you to go...
I don't want to dream too much
About tomorrows I can't know,
About a time when I may tell you that I love you so.

Just hold me in your arms and I'll try not to shiver,
Just find me a place in your heart.
Just please don't leave me lonely,
Or I just might fall apart.

You are like a precious gemstone, sparkling in my eyes,
Like gold at the end of a broken road,
Like the gentle waves of the ocean,
As the tide begins to rise.

To me, you're like a sunrise:
Soft hues and bright light, moving together in a slow dance.
I guess what I'm hoping for with all my heart,
Is that you'll give me more than just a chance.

So Close.

He holds me so close and gently he touches my tears.
He looks into my eyes and smiles at me with love,
And soon, I feel peace and I always feel welcome.
He thanks me for just being me
and gives me so much of what I really need.

I can't describe how special it is, this gift that is mine anytime,
But then he thanks me for the treasure he gives.
It doesn't make sense, but I know that it's right,
And it is I, who is so very thankful for him.

I feel like I have a real home, like I have my own family,
A private garden to cultivate and enjoy;
And when the storms come, we still keep blooming together.

Only the angels can see the full
magnitude of the love between him and me,
'Cause he holds me so close and gently he touches my tears,
And turns them from sad and angry streams
Into sparkling droplets of joy.

My Valentine.

Within that place where friendship had bloomed,
A simple hug all but consumed
My heart, with warmth and sincerity.

In that moment, I found my valentine,
A love that was lasting and all mine,
Something deeper than Cupid's arrows that pierced me.

Today I still find peace in his arms,
Free from the wounds of other's harms,
And a sense of soulful prosperity,
With the assurance that true love is real.

Our Time.

If I said I loved you a million times,
It could not reveal what you mean to me,
And if I wrote for you a million rhymes,
They could not express how I've been blessed
By having you here next to me.

The years go by so quickly and the seasons change.
No matter how we strive and try to rearrange
Our time, it presses on, but so does our love.

I'm having a hard time lately and God knows why,
Thinking about the time when one of us will have to say goodbye.
Let's treasure all these moments that we're here,
To hold each other dear.

And I will say 'I love you' a million times, and not in vain,
Because our hearts and souls are bound together
By love's precious chains.
Let's look into each other's eyes and smile,
'Cause we've still got a little while.

Once Upon A Time.

"... cast not your pearls before swine, lest they trample them under their feet, and turn again and rend you." Matthew 7:6, KJV

Once upon a time, I handed you some shining pearls,
Some precious jewels I had found inside myself.
You hesitated, but you took some, held them tenderly in your hand,
And admired them, cherishing them for a moment.

But to have really accepted them
would have been like poison for you,
So you tried and tried to gently give them back to me;
But every time you reached out toward me,
I tried to add one more,
Even larger and more beautiful than the others.

I wanted to impress you with a glimpse,
a token of all the treasures I held inside,
Because you seemed to truly value
what I thought might be beautiful,
About myself, and about life in general;
But more than that, I wanted to touch you,
To make you feel a warmth inside
because you were so precious and genuine to me
And I loved you so.

Anyway, I wouldn't take back the pearls,
and though I think you may have wanted to keep them,
And even perhaps hand me some of your own, you couldn't.
And the ones I had given you began burning your palms,
and so you had no choice

But to coldly,
ungraciously throw them back in my face and walk away.

As soon as I can stop my tears, I will look for them again.
Someday, I will gather them up
and put them in a safe, dark, place,
And I don't know when, or if, I will bring them out again,
And I may never hand them to anyone again.

There are a few missing that I'm sure you are unaware of,
But that I'm also sure you will find someday
in a pocket somewhere.
Some lonely day you may even find
one glimmering in a forgotten crevice of your heart.
And though 'happily ever after' is a harsh unreality,
that shining pearl may bring you a smile
And a tear, as you remember 'once upon a time.'

CHAPTER THREE
Spiritual

My intention with the following poems/lyrics is not to present an assortment of my beliefs, but rather to express my convictions through them. It is my hope that those who share similar convictions will find inspiration and comfort in them.

"God Will Be With Me."
(song lyrics)

Where is my heart and what is my song?
What do I see when my eyes close at night?
Resting in prayer, I whisper His name,
My body in darkness, my soul in the light.

(Chorus)
God will be with me, God will be with me.
He won't forsake me, or leave me alone.
God will be with me, right there beside me,
With me, each moment, guiding me on.

Where do I go and what steps do I take?
What do I do when sorrows abound?
Turning inside, I look upon Jesus,
Right there beside me, turning me around.

Where is my life and what fears control me?
What do I hear when silence rings deep?
Listening to Him, there's sweet, gentle music
Chiming what to let go of and what I must keep.

(Chorus)

Where is my end? What was my beginning?
What do I cling to in the light of today?
Reaching toward Him, He gives me His hand,
His love is ever present to show me the way.

(Chorus)

He Said.

"Be strong," He said, with His arms around our shoulders,
"Be strong," He said, with a smile upon His face.
"Find joy," He said, "amidst the tears you're weeping."
"Find faith," He said, "beyond this sickened human race."

"Find love," He said, "beyond the shadows of the darkness."
"Find peace," He said, with the twinkling of His eye.
"Find hope," He said, "within your doubts about tomorrow."
"Be strong," He said, "because all you can do is try."

"Rest In Me. (a song from above)"
(song lyrics)

"Come unto me, all ye that labour and are heavy laden, and I will give you rest." Matthew 11:28, KJV

Rest in me, rest in me -- I can give you peace.
Take my hand and understand that my love doesn't cease.
Believe in me, believe in me, and in time you'll see –
There's a way, in just today, to find serenity.

Accept my will, and let it spill into your thirsty soul.
Shed the tears behind the fears of what you can't control.

Reaching out, reaching out, you can then embrace
Simple mirth and human worth, the reflection of your face.
In the light, in the light, where faith and hope abound,
Honesty will set you free to a haven that is sound.

Though storms will come,
and sweltering sun may leave you tired and weak,
Let anger go, and then you'll know that what you really seek

Is:

Rest in me, rest in me, to accept my gift of peace,
To take my hand and to understand that my love doesn't cease.

CHAPTER FOUR
Family

For me, family is a treasure. I love each and every member of my large family. The following are some poems about various members. I hope you can relate to some of the substance in these writings. Also, I want to be clear that, although these particular poems address only a few of my family members, each one, living or deceased, holds a very special place in my heart.

Words From A Burdened One.

Must I just see the world through hazy eyes,
And try to hide what I can't disguise.
To see me struggle, to see me fall
For you, is maybe worst of all,
When life for me becomes stiffness and pain,
And you watch me reach for what I cannot gain.

But I do bring laughter and a sunny smile,
Love you can trust with every mile
That you carry me along.
And I have an encouraging song
That's not sad, inactive, or forlorn…
It's been sweet, rhythmic, and hopeful
Since I was born.

Understanding is hard for people to grasp,
When they feel their hands in my loose clasp,
When they see climbing, jumping children at play,
Or wrestle with my complaints all day.

No, I'm not what any of us had planned,
But, please, don't be afraid to hold my hand.

Dear Brother, Elmer.

It was you who taught me to ride a bike and to make a slingshot.
It was you who helped and encouraged me
to climb into the tree house you had built.
It was you who threw down your bat and glove
When the neighbor kids wanted you in the game, but not me.

It was you who stood up for me when no one else would.
It was you and I who shared so many private lunches
with our mother,
And sat on either side of her again two days before she died –
And, later, it was you who couldn't help but cry when you viewed
her lifeless body.

But it was always you who made me laugh
at silly things gone wrong,
Who showed me how to shoot marbles into little shoebox houses,
And how to make mountains and roads and bridges in the sand.
And, yes, it was you who taunted and teased me,
and played tricks on me for fun…

But I remember all that lovingly
because it seemed you were always there for me,
So much older, but yet so young.
Remember the magnificent snow fort you built,
where you let me hide and play?
Remember how my small feet could walk on top of the snow,
but you sank to your waist one day?

It's no wonder I felt like your faithful squire
as the years went rolling by;

And it's no wonder why you're so special to me,
Now that so much more time has come and gone.

We were the babies of the family,
you and I, and perhaps not so ironically,
The last in line, as we walked embracing each other,
following Dad's casket out of the church.
So many are the fond and loving memories I have of you,
my dear brother,
'Cause in the simplest ways
you showed me where the best stepping stones were
Beneath so many threatening streams;
And, today it is you who I am so proud of and grateful for!

Mom In August.

If she were here, she'd be so busy crocheting
blankets, bonnets, and booties
For her great-grandchildren,
Canning peaches and making jam,
Gathering vegetables and tending flowers,
In the hot summer sun.

She'd be baking for birthdays and planning for fall,
Fixing big, Sunday dinners for all who would show.
She'd be tired and cranky from all that she'd do,
But then smiling and lovingly, she'd give something to you,
To brighten your day or to lighten your load...
To change you for life.

A Tribute To Mom and Dad.

"Be sure to kiss them now, every time you see them,
And give them the hugs you didn't give in years gone by,"
I tell myself, and my heart tells me too,
Because winter has bloomed in their tired eyes.

I wonder if they know how much I've loved them,
How pain, and anger at life, made me afraid to reach
Toward loving hands that used to guide me,
Toward wholesome hearts that used to teach.

They are the roots that always nourished
The wandering child, who learned too slow
That these two souls were my beginnings, that these two lives
Hold all my winnings...
That, in this life, is all I need to know.

And I wonder if they know how proud I am of each of them
For fighting hard life's losing battles,
for keeping faith, for moving on;
So many things I need to tell them,
So little time to try to right the wrongs.

Oh, so kind-hearted, so forgiving,
they've always been a hero's song:
Of love and laughter 'midst the chaos,
amidst the twilight in my eyes.
I don't know how to say to Mommy
that I'm forever nestled near her heart,
Or how to say to him, "I see it now, Daddy,
What you've both given from the start."

Heartfelt Thoughts

I only wish you could see yourselves the way I do:
Brave and beautiful, living your lives the best you could;
You lived better than most who lived with much less adversity,
And you were never less than anyone,
as you strove so hard to be so good.

Wintry eyes and wintry smiles
now trudge on toward the dawn of spring.
Don't cry, Mama.
Don't fret, Papa.
Life is beautiful.
God has made it so.

And you... you are my resources besides Him:
My heroes, the passions that drive all of my successes...
Please, know this well, for my sake, before it's time to go.

Ruth M. Clancy

A Poem For Tela.

Oh, my dear daughter, I don't know what to say;
I feel so broken when you hurt, I just close my eyes and pray.
Oh, my sweet girl, you will always be my child,
And although you're a young woman now,
you are so delicate and mild.

But if anyone has courage, then surely it is you,
'Cause whatever is the right thing, that's the thing you try to do.
I wish we all could grow up just by wishing on a star,
But, if so, you needn't wish to be good, 'cause you already are.

Sometimes life gives us many things we just don't understand,
And we become so disheartened
when they're not what we had planned;
But just keep hanging in there, and you will bloom and grow,
But only time can teach you that; no one can tell you so.

I know that they're so heavy, all the burdens that you bear,
And it's sometimes hard to notice that God is everywhere;
But when I look out at my sunflower, it often helps me see
How wonderful and gracious God has always been to me.

And when I sprinkle it with water, I can see a bright rainbow;
It's then I always think of you, and then it really starts to show...
All the beauty and the sweetness, and the love that life can bring,
And all the prayers that God has answered,
in the midst of everything.

Heartfelt Thoughts

So remember, my dear daughter,
though many dreams will fade away,
That there are many all around us that have come true today —
'Cause you remind me of that sunflower strong,
that the wind its stem must bend,
But even more so, you are that rainbow,
a loving promise God did send.

Ruth M. Clancy

To My Brother, Eugene.

And so, my brother, just want you to know
how I've loved you as I have grown;
You gave me books when I was young;
you always gave kindness, sweet music, and songs.
You have always been the best to us all,
I was so happy to hear you each time you called.

And one day, when I was just three,
at our mother I was mad as could be;
I told her she was way too mean,
that I was going to Syracuse to live with Gene.

And so, my brother, I love you still...
I always have and I always will!

CHAPTER FIVE
Miscellaneous

The following is poetry that doesn't necessarily fit into a specific category. Nonetheless, the words are from the heart, and written at various times during my life, about different events and feelings I have experienced.

Ruth M. Clancy

Memorial Day.
(Inspired by James)

"Why do they burn the flag?" he asked, with teardrops in his eyes.
"I have that picture on my hat, with an eagle standing by;
And there lies my brother, a thousand flags all around,
Some are flying high, others stuck in the ground.

And look at all those flowers, all the flowers in full bloom,
But me, I dare not touch them, for fear of all the doom."

Then he smiled and said to me,
"I will wave all my flags really high,
For all the world to see,
I will put them in the rafters, not one or two, but three;

And I will sing and shout and clap my hands,
As the soldiers, they walk by.
I will wave mine really high," he said,
"So that they may never die."

He Sang.

He sang "Happy Birthday" to himself, that 90-year-old man;
He sang and resounded over a huge crowd of voices,
And I heard him; I heard his pronounced chanting
From over 50 feet away, and, perhaps, the whole valley heard.
Perhaps the angels heard and carried his silly echoes
To my mom's previously deaf ears, and perhaps she smiled,
Or chuckled, as I did, along with at least a hundred others...
Perhaps, you heard him too.

Sounds of Night.

A mournful train echoes its moans through the valley,
Its loud, rumbling engine sounding
as if it's coming down Main Street.
The quiet night air and the frantic chirping
of a bat are doomed by the intrusion,
Along with the tolling church bell.
Yet, for me, the distant train that sounds so close,
Soothes my memory back to a happier time.
Soon the whistling and the rumbling will fade,
And the night will resume whatever song it will sing,
Or it may lapse into silence,
Perhaps interrupted only by the whooshing of a car passing by.

Does anyone hear?
Does anyone care about the sounds of night?
Or the lack thereof?
But, wait...here comes another train.

Into September.

Thunder rolls faintly in the distance, momentarily blocking out
the sound of the cricket multitudes; their song began,
they will be singing into September.
But my thoughts pause and I remember how I miscarried a baby,
Some 27 years ago.
I still have the gift a friend gave to me then,
tucked away in a keepsake box,
Along with my daughter's baby shoes and my mother's obituary.
How peaceful is this night, even though it may storm,
And here I am, tucked into a cozy cottage,
with my fan softly humming,
My clock gently ticking, and the love of my life sleeping soundly.
Soon I too will be slumbering in the moist,
warm darkness of this August night.
Tomorrow will be hot, and thundershowers will come and go,
But the crickets will still be singing... into September.

Ruth M. Clancy

One November Morning.

One November morning I woke up after a treacherous storm.
The snow was new and fresh;
the ice was smooth, crisp, and easily broken.
The atmosphere was gray and white... cold and calm.
Though I shivered, there was peace,
and though I ached, there was softness.

No bird's song, just silence filled the air, a restful, relieving quiet,
Dancing in a gentle wind, pressing against a solemn sky.
And I drank everything in, in small sips, and became nourished.

Though my energy and my spirits were still low,
I found the courage to open my eyes,
Even though I was still frightened --
and that's what made the difference:
To be able to close them for rest and not for fear.

And though the storm is not forgotten, or its harshness and pain,
One November morning its fierce intensity did not filter through,
And though I still hurt,
feeling alive and capable was all that mattered.

Maria.

Maria works in the fields today, aching in the autumn cold,
Just trying to get the job done, just trying not to grow old.
Maria's kids are crying, scared, and alone in the Florida sun;
Somebody might snatch them away from here --
there's no place to go, no place to run.

Maria went to the food factory -- for 14 hours she earned her pay,
But on the way home, her eyelids got heavy,
and a big tree got in her way.
Now she'll be all right, though she's hurting,
and her sister's got a bad broken arm,
But the money's gone just from circumstance,
and everybody's leaving the farm.

So Maria heads back south with her sister
and the lover who came with her too,
But he gets scared and leaves her cold --
heads for Canada, without having a clue.
Where he goes is just a rumored place,
a mythical haven, a northern dream,
So he runs with no skills, no money,
no English, like a runaway slave caught in midstream.

And there's no job for Maria in Florida,
and to stay legal, she's got to pay.
How will she and her family survive,
whether or not they can stay?
But their chances are still better
in this world than the world from which they came.
There's not much in life sadder than Maria's tears,
nothing more dignified than her story -- her name.

Ruth M. Clancy

We need to remember her sorrow,
her pride, her dreams, her smile.
We need to reach out and embrace her with love,
if only for a little while.
And we may never know what happens to Maria,
or the thousands like her that we never see,
Or, when we do, they become a visible nuisance
or a political issue over which to disagree –
But Maria is not an issue, she is simply you and me.

And Maria works in the fields today, aching in the autumn cold,
Just trying to get the job done, just trying not to grow old.

About the Author

Ruth M. Clancy lives in a small village in Western New York. She has been writing poetry since her teenage years and holds a Bachelor's degree in English and a Master's in Education from Nazareth College of Rochester. Ruth writes when she's moved by strong emotions, using poetry to express thoughts she finds difficult to speak aloud. After years of writing privately, she was inspired to finally share her work. Heartfelt Thoughts is her first published book.

www.ingramcontent.com/pod-product-compliance
Lightning Source LLC
Chambersburg PA
CBHW020810160426
43192CB00006B/516